A Nurse's Guide To Beating
DEPRESSION

Books That Speak To The SOUL

Dr. Paul J. Young

A Nurse's Guide To Beating

Beating

DEPRESSION

Dr. Paul J. Young

A
TOTAL RELIEF SYSTEMS
publication

DRPAULYOUNG.COM

1

Depressed Nurses…REALLY?

———————————————

SO YOU ARE A NURSE. That means that you are an awesome person who dispenses comfort, compassion and caring love even without a prescription.

You are the hero of the medical profession, the heart of healthcare, and there to give hope.

Someone said that if you save one life you are a hero, but if you save hundreds of lives, you are a nurse!

You are an angel with a stethoscope.

And there are nearly 3 million of you in the USA.

Yet, TOO MANY NURSES SUFFER FROM DEPRESSION (9% of everyday citizens are depressed but **18%** if nurses are depressed). Sad, isn't it, that depression is EPIDEMIC among nurses.

Did you get that…**epidemic!**

So what you are struggling with is not unique. Too many nurses get on the elevator each day, going up to their unit to faithfully serve.

Your shift hasn't started yet, but there is an uneasy sadness invading your mind, spreading its roots throughout your thoughts. But you have to hang in there, keep at it and help people. After all you are a nurse.

No one knows how you struggle. You smile, laugh with your team members, but still, underneath the facade, there it is, that depression.

Will it ever go away?

You've tried pills and therapy. But nothing seems to quiet the emptiness you feel deep inside.

Nothing.

Until now.

I am going to take you on a journey through THREE DOORS that could very well change your life…for good. By the time you go through door three you will finally discover why you feel alienated deep inside, lost and unsatisfied.

My goal is not to bring you back to normal, but to take you a number of notches above that, to a place of inner pleasure and joy - that kind of joy that bubbles forth from hope and peace.

Ah. That's what you want, don't you? So keep reading. Hope is just around the corner.

And…

Thanks for being a nurse! What a beautiful career you chose. My purpose is to help you to enjoy every moment of that career!

2

Only $2.99

____

YOU ARE DEPRESSED.   That's why you bought this book, hoping for a cure…for $2.99 (more if you bought the paperback). And, you smiled when you paid less than a three dollars for some help that you would pay a thousand dollars for, maybe a lot more.

And, it is true, you may have spent thousands on therapy and pills…and are still depressed.

What could this book like this do for you?

You laugh.

Kind of stupid, isn't it, believing that I could help you when no one else has?

Or is it?

Maybe I know something that you don't know, something that will take you deep inside your inner self, shine a light on it and help you to fix it.

What if?

So you wonder if I can really fix you…for good, or whether you will keep searching for some lost formula, some hidden elixir that will make everything right again.

Yep, a $2.99 cure - A NURSE'S GUIDE TO BEATING DEPRESSION, for so little, yet with great promise.

Frankly, it's not a $2.99 cure. It cost me years of study - over seven years of academic study after college, all the time, the tens of thousands of dollars I spent to learn what I know, as well as all the decades of experience.

This is no $2.99 cure - at least for me.

Yet, as a nurse, you get in on what I know, all the years of experience helping people around the world, thousands of people, one on one, in small groups and in crowds sometimes larger than a thousand, as I taught people principles about life and how to find happiness, peace and joy.

Today, a great host of people have experienced deep changes in their lives because I shared with them what I believe to be the great secret to a happy life.

And I want to share it with you, all for so little.

Quite a deal, isn't it?

I trade all I have learned, all the lessons I have taught people about how to break through one's depression, all the steps that are so often lost and never talked about in most therapist's sessions. All of it, all of me for only $2.99.

It's a steal!

But not if you stop reading. You need to follow me all the way through this short but powerful read.

Why will it be powerful, the kind of power that could make a difference in your life?

When I studied psychology to get my doctorate from Biola University (in conjunction with Rosemead School Of Psychology, Talbot School of Theology, as well as other visiting professors from great graduate schools), I began to realize that too often the books I read, the leaders of various psychological theories I studied, did not take people deep enough.

Because of that, their methods of therapy, though good, did not understand the core of humanity, the essential construct that makes a human a human - the soul.

This is what you will find so different in this book, my insight into the SOUL, your soul.

But more of this later.

In this book I will take you through three steps - through three doors to healing that will cure your depression.

The **FIRST STEP** or door will be based on cognitive therapy which, I believe, is the first great step to find healing. It is here that you work on thoughts and actions.

But I want to take you beyond this, beyond where most cognitive-behavioral therapists take you.

In the **SECOND STEP** and door, I will help you understand what beliefs are truly foundational to your life. Beliefs are thoughts that are rooted and thus impact any thoughts or actions you take.

This section could very well open a new door for you and set you on a journey that will help to end your depression as you examine your beliefs.

But this still is not good enough. We want to defeat your depression once and for all, or at least give you the tools to handle any time you begin to feel a gripping sadness and hopelessness.

In STEP THREE, or door 3, we will finally take you to a place where you can REALLY, FINALLY get healed. I will help you journey to the essential core of who you are and how this core can be renewed, refreshed and flow with continuous joy, happiness, hope and peace.

It will be incredible!

All for $2.99! - this Nurse's Guide to Defeating Depression.

But you have to stay with me even when you feel a little resistant.

Make a commitment to take my three steps and go through the 3 doors I ask you to open and move through.

I will have assignments I want you to do, things to repeat, and thoughts to ponder. Work through these, and in a matter of days, maybe even today, the vice-grip hold of your depression will begin to lessen, and soon finally go away…

For Good!

PART ONE
Door Number 1
GETTING UNSTUCK

1

Breaking Loose

LOOK AT THE PICTURE. You can see the indecision on her face, can't you? Let's call her Darcy.

Darcy has been stuck, sitting in that chair for days, weeks, maybe months. For most of the time the door was shut, and the room was dark.

But now Darcy picks up my book. She begins to read, and as she does, a faint glimmer of hope splashes across her face. She gets up, opens the door, thinking:

Shall I go through that door, leave my safety in this dark space and venture out into another room or place, shine the light on my depression and look at it in a totally different way?

Getting unstuck.

Breaking loose, as a nurse,

from the chains

that have bound you to your

depression.

This is what this section is about.

2

Misinterpretation of Events

OST PEOPLE SINCERELY BELIEVE THAT:

Events = Emotion

This belief keeps them stuck in their depression, in the darkness of hopelessness and defeat. If you are depressed, you probably believe that this equation is true.

And it does make sense.

After all, you are a nurse and have invested a lot of time in study. "Shouldn't I blame the things that are happening to me for my depression," you ask?

You have a patient, for whom you have invested a lot of time, die, leaving you baffled, upset and defeated. Or someone you love leaves you. These events seem to cause the sadness you feel. You are down, depressed and anxious about your life.

Then it may be that you find you have cancer, lose a lot of money, a job, or someone says something hateful to you, and on and on. These are events that seem to cause emotional breakdown.

Yet, and listen to me, you must get what I am to say, or you will be stuck in your depression.

Events = Emotion
is a FALSE EQUATION

You see, no event can make you depressed.

Shocked? I hope so. I want to grab your attention and let you in on the secret too many do not know. Events do not cause your emotional feelings but rather your INTERPRETATION of the events.

Stay with me so you can understand this.

In the first door, Darcy was stuck in her prison of hopelessness. Why? She blamed an event. But it wasn't the event that chained her to that chair and kept her in darkness. It was her INTERPRETATION of that event.

What event? It doesn't matter what event it may be. Events DO NOT have power over you. They are just happenings that cascade through our lives. The thing that does have power over you are your THOUGHTS about that event.

Since this is true we can adjust our equation from:

$$\text{Events} = \text{Emotion}$$

To...

Events + INTERPRETATION
(of those events) = Emotion

Listen. It is YOUR INTERPRETATION of the event that makes you depressed, swamped by hopelessness and sorrow. So then we can clearly state:

**CHANGE YOUR INTERPRETATION
AND YOU WILL CHANGE YOUR EMOTION
(feelings of depression)**

That's it!

"Ya, but," you say. "You don't know what happened to me, the rejection I feel, the money I lost, the person I loved who died or rejected me or all the stress on my job."

Give me any event and I can show you how to interpret it so you feel better.

Now I'm not saying that there should never be a time where you feel down, where sorrow swamps you and you feel emotionally shattered.

I know. I lost a wife to cancer after over four decades of marriage. I have had to battle 3 kinds of cancer that could have killed me. I had a financial advisor steal nearly $100,000 from my investments and battled through disappointments of all kinds.

And there are times I get depressed.

Is this shocking since I am writing this book on how to cure it?

Let's get real. Depression happens. Yet, we don't have to get trapped in a dark prison of depression for long. We can break out if we know what to do.

And what is it?

CHANGE YOUR *INTERPRETATION*
AND YOU WILL CHANGE YOUR FEELINGS

**Your feelings are held hostage
by what you think and what you do.**

How do you change your interpretations?

Realize that INTERPRETATIONS are only THOUGHTS that come to you because of an event. Something happens, your best friend turns against you, and you start thinking… thinking…thinking. These thoughts are interpretations of the event, interpretations that will move you into depression or keep you from being totally devastated.

Let me take some events and show you how to change your thoughts from being destructive to thoughts that will bring hope. We call this flipping (like flipping a switch from negative thoughts that will swamp you to thoughts that will encourage you).

This is also called reframing your thoughts so that the outcome will be one of hope instead of a gripping sadness and hopelessness.

The following are illustrations of how to do it. You can find a whole book I wrote that has thousands of illustrations on hundreds of subjects. It's called: *Dr. Paul's FEELING GOOD ToolKit*.

You can find it at <u>DrPaulYoung.com</u>

Read through the next few pages - illustrations of how you can change your INTERPRETATION and thus change your emotion.

EVENT	INTERPRETATIONS FLIP IT REFRAMING	EMOTION
Cancer	Why is this happening to me?	Depression
	How can I go on?	Hopelessness
	I might die.	Grief
	God must hate me.	Disappointment
	I am going to learn from this experience.	Peace
	Thank God for the many people who are going to help me. I'm so lucky!	Joy. Gratitude

EVENT	INTERPRETATIONS	EMOTION
	If I die I'd go to heaven.	Hope
Lost my job	We are going to go broke and lose our home.	Depression
	This is unfair.	Anger
	I am going to work hard and find another job	Encouragement
	I am thankful for the job I did have.	Gratitude
Investment down	I won't be able to retire.	Hopelessness
	Who is going to take care of me?	Confusion
	I give up.	Depression
	Stocks will come back. They always do.	Hope.
	Delayed retirement doesn't mean I can't enjoy my life.	Encouragement

EVENT	INTERPRETATIONS FLIP IT, REFRAMING	EMOTION
Problem Children	Why did I ever have kids?	Anger
	I feel so rejected.	Depression
	They don't treat me right.	Resentment

	No matter what they do, I will show my love to them.	Determination
	Even though they are not behaving the right way, I choose to love them and thank God for them.	Joy Peace
Health Problems	I'm sick of being sick!	Depression
	Why me?	Hopelessness
	I feel miserable all the time.	Resentment
	Why does God let bad things happen to good people? This sucks!	Doubt
	At least I'm alive!	Hope
	I will not let my sickness define who I am.	Determination
	I will focus on the many other good things I have and not my sickness.	Joy Gratitude
	What can I learn from my sickness?	Anticipation
People Problems	Why do they act like jerks?	Anger

	I will never talk with them again.	Resentment Bitterness
	I have no true friends.	Depression
	I will continue to be a friend.	Determination
	Though others may reject me, I accept myself and know that I am a good person.	Hope
	I will find a good friend if I keep being a loving, friendly person.	Happiness
Father is a jerk.	Why did I get such a jerk of a father?	Depression
	When will he ever learn to treat me right?	Misery
	My dad's a jerk, but I still love him.	Hope
	I will always show outward love to my father through my actions and words.	Determination
	Though my dad acts like a jerk at times, I choose to thank God for my dad.	Joy Gratitude

Work Problems	I hate this job!	Anger Frustration Disgust
	I'll never get ahead.	Depression
	It's 12 years before I can retire.	Hopelessness
	The pay is miserable.	Discouragement
	At least I have a job!	Gratefulness
	If I am patient, I can find a better job.	Hope
	Though I have a sad job, I choose to be happy.	Joy
	The pain I feel is going to make me a better person.	Peace

EVENT	INTERPRETATIONS FLIP IT, REFRAMING	EMOTION
My husband died	I can't make it.	Hopelessness
	I wish I were dead.	Depression
	I hurt so much.	Grief
	"God. Why did you let this happen?"	Anger
	Thank you God for letting us live this long together.	Gratitude

EVENT	INTERPRETATIONS FLIP IT, REFRAMING	EMOTION
	I will miss him terribly, but I will make it and find joy again.	Hope
	He's in heaven and having a great time.	Joy
I have no real friends	I'm worthless.	Depression
	No one likes me.	Worthlessness
	Nothing will ever change.	Hopelessness
	Until I find a friend, I will be a friend to myself.	Peace
	I will go to church and join a group.	Hope
	I will stop moping and start coping!	Determination
	I will make someone a great friend!	Confidence Joy
EVENT	**INTERPRETATIONS FLIP IT, REFRAMING**	**EMOTION**
Look how much I weigh!	I'm a failure.	Failure
	To be liked, I must be thin.	Hopelessness
	Fat is ugly.	Depression
	Fat is beautiful!	Joy

	I choose to be happy though fat!	Glad
	My joy is not dependent on how much I weigh.	Peace
Constant problems	Why is life so hard?	Disappointment
	Nothing seems to turn out right.	Hopelessness
	I just feel such a weight.	Despair
	God is unfair.	Anger
	These weighty problems are really exciting challenges.	Hope
	Anything is possible if I don't quit.	Encouragement
	Complaining only brings misery. I will stop complaining for a day.	Peace
	I will quit fixing the blame and fix the problem.	Confidence

Now write out the events that you are going through right now. Take each event and come up with some interpretations that will bring hope.

As you do this, always tell yourself the truth. You are not trying to distort what is happening to you, only seeking to come up with another way of looking at it, a way that will bring courage, hope and even joy.

Remember, it is not the event that has brought the depression but the way you interpreted that event.

Practice now:

Name the EVENT that is depressing you. Come up with some INTERPRETATIONS - ways of viewing that event or happening in a way that will produce emotions that lift you up rather than defeat you.

Remember:

CHANGE YOUR *INTERPRETATION* AND YOU WILL CHANGE HOW YOU FEEL

3

Become An Actor or Actress

IN COGNITIVE-BEHAVIORAL THERAPY, it is not just **THOUGHTS** that change how you feel but **ACTIONS**. When you take action steps, something is triggered in the brain. Your thoughts begin to change relative to the action steps you take.

It's magical!

For example, when you are depressed, put a big smile on your face, or laugh. These action steps actually trigger a response in your brain that sends new messages to your emotions and you actually feel better.

It's not that you want to do something that is not in line with the truth. Yes, you are depressed. But your desired end is to stop that depression. How? Change your thoughts and your actions.

When you act in a way in line with how you WANT to feel (though you are not feeling that way now) you will, with certainty, change how you feel.

Many depressed people slump when they sit or stand.

ACTION: Stand or sit up straight. Put your shoulders back like you are confident.

Other depressed people breathe shallow breaths.

ACTION: Take deep breaths. Hold the breath for a few seconds, then let it out slowly. Do this for three minutes.

Many depressed people never smile or laugh.

ACTION: Put a big smile on your face and laugh for one minute. Laughing actually massages your internal organs and releases a natural drug that makes you happy. So laugh!

You may say that you don't feel like it.

Of course you don't. That is why these action steps are so important. They force you to do something that you do not want to do, but in doing it, bring about change - a release, even for a moment, from your depression.

Remember: When you connect this action with a change of your interpretation, it's powerful!

Look at some examples below:

EVENT	ACTION	EMOTION
LOST JOB	Smile	Hopeful
	Look for job	Determination
	Focus on heart's desires for job	Excitement
	Laugh/Dance	Joy
	Relax/Deep breaths	Peace
	Go for a walk	Calm
HUSBAND IS A JERK	Write out his 20 positive attributes and share them with him	Caring
	Write out a list of 10 ways you can please him and do them one at a time	Determination
	Smile/Laugh/Dance	Joy
	Focus on fun with girlfriends	Anticipation
	Counter his jerkiness with love	Brave
	Give a blessing for a curse	Love
NEWS IS BAD	Turn off the news	Less anxiety

	Play uplifting music	Joy
	Focus on the good news	Hopeful
	Google good news	Inspired
	Turn on the radio and listen to music	Calming
	Laugh for one minute. Do this 10 times today	Pleasure
CANCER	Smile. Say: "I've got cancer but cancer doesn't have me!"	Determination
	Cry (It is never good to repress actions that flow from a terrible event. Grief, anger, anxiety, depression, loneliness and other emotional responses are healthy. They become UNHEALTHY, though when we hang on to them for an extended period of time. You must be honest and truthful in your approach to writing out interpretations and actions)	Release anxiety
	Shout: "I'm going to win! Cancer is going to lose!"	Hope
	Laugh	Daring

	Write a list of things and people you are grateful for	Thanksgiving
	Become part of a support group	Encouragement
INVESTMENT DOWN	Practice deep breathing	Peace
	Smile	Joy
	Laugh	Optimistic
	Shout: "I'm down but not out!"	Hopeful
	Go for a walk	Calming
PROBLEMS WITH FAMILY, WORK, FRIENDS, MOTHER, HEALTH	Stop complaining!	Relaxed
	Get off your butt and do something!	Determination
	Write out a list of your problems and what you plan on DOING about it	Hopeful
	Quite bitching and start blessing	Joyful
	Focus on blessing	Gratefulness
	Write out a list of all the good things about your family, work, friends, mother, health, etc.	Positive
	Smile, laugh, breathe, shout, dance	Liberated

	Walk, eat good foods for your brain (omega 3), build strong social networks, walk, workout, listen to music	All these things bring a calm to the brain and peace to the soul
HUSBAND DIED	Cry	Release tension
	Smile	Gratefulness
	Say: " Thank God he isn't suffering anymore."	Thankful
	List all the good attributes he had	Grateful
	Say: "I will make it."	Determination
	Buy a bird, dog, cat, fish	Fills up that lonely space
	Be with family/friends	Calm
TIRED	Breathe	Peace
	Smile	Joy
	Take a nap	Hope
	Go for a slow walk	Energizes
	Eat foods that give energy	Determination

These are just some sample ways to use ACTION steps to break you out of the prison of depression.

Now, write out some action steps that will help you break free from your depression.

EVENT.	ACTION	EMOTION
1.		
2.		
3.		
4.		

This is not easy to do. But if you are going to be joyful again, work at it, and success will be yours! You will finally not only be cured, but know how to cure yourself when depression comes knocking at your door again.

THOUGHTS + ACTIONS = EMOTION

Change your thoughts and actions and you will FEEL better again.[1]

---

[1] If you want to go deeper into this topic, you can read through my **Dr. Paul's TOTAL Relief - Depression.** It is a series of books, workbooks and YES! Cards that will help you immensely.

Also, my book, **Dr. Paul's FEELING GOOD ToolKit** lists hundreds of areas that open the door to depression and how to THINK and ACT in each situation. It will be a big help to you.

All these books, if bought together (10 books total), will cost you a fraction of the fees you would pay if you had a personal session with me or any psychotherapist.

PART 2

Door Number 2
EMBRACING LOVE

1

Core Beliefs

IN DOOR NUMBER 1, WE SAW DARCY MOVING from the chair of depression that held her in a prison of darkness and defeat. That ended when she opened the door and let some light on her situation. From there she learned how to have proper THOUGHTS and ACTIONS. Learning this began to bring an end to her depression.

But there was a reoccurring difficulty, her core beliefs.

Beliefs are simply thoughts that are rooted, and when one of your core beliefs is at odds with what is true, it will sabotage your thoughts and thus your emotions.

For example, if Darcy felt that she was not worthy of being loved, then that belief would sabotage all her work in developing thoughts that would get her out of her depression.

Some core beliefs are:

BELIEFS	FEELINGS
I am good	Competent
I am bad	Miserable
As a person, I am significant	Loved
I'm nobody	Worthless
I can weather any difficulty	Confidence
I am loved (by God and others)	Secure
I belong	Acceptance
No one loves me for who I am	Hopelessness
I am competent	Confidence
I'm a failure	Shame
I'm ugly	Useless
I'm fun to be with	Joy
I can make it through any circumstance	Hopeful
Nothing ever turns out right	Despair
Life is difficult, but I have help from God and others	Determination

Dig deep and come up with some of your core beliefs and write what kind of feelings those beliefs are producing.

BELIEFS   **FEELINGS**

1.

2.

3.
4.

5.

6.

7.

9.

10.

2

THE GREATEST CORE BELIEF

THERE ARE MANY GOOD AND WORTHWHILE CORE BELIEFS that can help you break out of depression and find relief.

If you believe that you are a person worth loving, and feel that love, it means that there are thoughts that are rooted deep in your heart. These thoughts that you have interpret reality, telling you that you are a person of worth, a person of significance and a person who has value.

"SOMEONE LOVES ME!" your heart screams out.

You know it. It is a settled fact. There is proof. My father, mother, husband, wife, friends, relatives and work associates love me.

It may not be all of them. It never is. But SOMEONE loves me.   There is ample evidence, enough to make this a settled truth, a BELIEF.

You see, the **ONE CORE BELIEF** THAT CHANGES EVERYTHING IS:

LOVE!

THIS FOUNDATION BELIEF IS THE MOST VITAL CORE BELIEF. The person who is loved will always find a way to smile, to break through the clouds of trouble, conflict and disaster, and find joy.

Isn't this what you want with all your heart?

Of course!

And believe me, I know how to get you there, not because I'm so smart, but because I know the path, the narrow path to take you there, the path that will bring you to the CURE FOR YOUR DEPRESSION.

This is why I wrote this guide for you as a nurse. I want you to be free from this crippling emotion.

As I have said before, there are many other paths that can bring some relief. You can change your THOUGHTS and

ACTIONS and learn how to INTERPRET any event so you can change your feelings.

But that will only take you so far. Stepping through door 1, and finally getting unstuck, breaking out of the prison of misinterpretations that have kept you behind the bars of darkness and despair, is great. Can it be better?

Yes it can!

Too often people only go this far and never experience the totality of joy, hope and peace they were made to feel. Why? They do not have a good foundational belief that someone loves them deeply and feels that they are valuable, significant and important.

This is why this core belief of LOVE is so important.

Let me help you understand it so that you can move through this door and fully embrace this belief, a belief that can be yours…guaranteed!

Darcy went through the door of love and found something surprising. You can find it too!

Our hearts ache to be fully loved - totally, completely.

There are three different types of love.

1. **I love you "if" kind of love.** "If you will do this for me, I will love you." This is purely conditional love. It puts you under the microscope and examines everything you are and do.

2. **I love you "because of" kind of love.** This is another conditional kind of love, but better than the "if" kind. It goes this way: "I love you because you are beautiful." But what happens if in an accident that beauty is marred? Love then evaporates. Or..."I love you because of your sense of humor." Yet, what occurs if this person suffers some kind of mental injury either by accident or disease? Are they still loved?

There is nothing wrong with loving a person because of beauty, humor, or any other positive trait. But this can't be a foundational and enduring kind of love.

3. **I love you "no matter what" kind of love.** Now this kind of love will last. We want to be loved this way, that no matter what happens, that person who declared their love for us will keep on loving us..."no matter what."

This is the kind of love that sacrifices for the person loved.

You remember Darcy?   Her fiancee left her for another woman. Why? His love was an "if" kind of love as he found another woman who gave HIM what he wanted.

This kind of love is selfish and self-centered. When Darcy's fiancee left her, he, in fact, showed that he never ever really loved Darcy.

Thank God the marriage never happened. Darcy would have had to live with a selfish, self-centered person the rest of her life - or until they divorced.

Once she realized this, she was able to take this terrible event, being left just weeks before the wedding, and see the good that came from it.

She was saved from years of misery!

The problem lies in this: Most humans are weak and imperfect. Thus their love is imperfect.

Where, then, can we find a love that is worth trusting, giving our lives to it without fear of being let down?

I'm sure that, as a nurse, you would love to find the answer to this question.

Read on.

3

GOD LOVES
YOU!

DARCY WAS ENGAGED TO THE LOVE OF HER LIFE. Then, just weeks before her marriage, this one she loved so much ran off with another woman, devastating her. "How could he do this," she sobbed? And through it all she began to wonder if anyone would ever love her again.

"Can anyone truly love me?"

That is a question we all ask at times. If we do not feel someone loves us, our hearts will ache most of our lives, chained to thoughts of inadequacy and fear.

So many die of a broken heart because they do not feel loved.

Is that you? Do you know that someone truly loves you? And…are you worth being loved?

You see the bold statement at the head of this chapter - God loves YOU!. But is that true? Is that only kind of like a Santa Claus myth that is just a feel good story that is not in line with reality?

Does God really love you?

Don't shove this question aside thinking that you are not interested at all in religion. To sweep God from your thoughts ultimately gets rid of all meaning and purpose in life. Why are you here? Who made you? Are you only a composite of organisms that came from an impersonal universe?

If you believe this, look at my book, *If There Is A God, Whose God is God?* It will help you think through you and God in a very logical way. I think you will like it.

This will open your heart to a love that can change your life.

The Holy Scriptures say: *GOD IS LOVE.*

This is essentially who he is…PURE LOVE.

And it's not the kind of love that is an "if" or a "because of" kind of love. Yes, it is true that God gives us laws and principles to live by, but only because he loves us. He never says: "You screw up, and I will hate you."

Never!

The Scriptures state:

> God **PROVED HIS LOVE** FOR US that while we were sinners (doing things that are wrong - things that hurt us and others), Christ DIED for us.
>
> Romans 5

Now that's the kind of love to build your life on, the kind to believe in.

God's love is ALWAYS giving.

> God so loved the world that he **GAVE** his only begotten Son.
>
> John 3

"Yet," people say, "if God loved me, why did this horrible thing happen?"

It's like Darcy saying: "If God loved me, why did he let my fiancee leave me just weeks before our marriage?"

You already know the answer, don't you?

You see what kind of jerk her fiancee was and how that marriage would have hurt Darcy. So GOD, IN LOVE, SAVED HER from what would have been a miserable marriage.

There is the age old question that states: "If God loves me and also has all power to stop anything, why did he let this horrible thing (like cancer, death of a child, loss of job, accident that left permanent scars, rape, divorce, etc.) happen to me?

First, God is love.

Second, God is all powerful.

Realize that God often does not stop our suffering and pain because HE DIDN'T STOP HIS SUFFERING and pain. Why? Suffering on his part and ours can be redemptive and bring about eternal and glorious changes both to us and others.

This is why in the Catholic and some other churches Jesus Christ is still on the cross in full display to all who enter.

Why? How grotesque!

Really?

Jesus said:

> *Greater love has no one for another than a person who gives his life for his friend.*

John 15

This is how much God loves you and me. God GAVE HIS ALL that we might find life to the full.

It is so important to understand God's love. If you do not grasp it and bank your life on it, you may ALWAYS struggle with some form of hopelessness and depression.

Yes, you can practice reinterpreting every event so that your feelings will change. Great! But that is not enough. If you want to move into a deeper kind of joy and inner happiness, you need to embrace the LOVE OF GOD.

I have sent people to a Catholic Church to spend time before the crucifix. I ask them to spend at least 15 minutes drinking in the love of God.

Go ahead, touch his wounds like Thomas did. It was in the touching of the wounds of Christ that he found new life, hope and even a new mission that drove him to India to share the good news about the love of God.

When a person goes into a Catholic Church they will see a red light (a candle) burning. This means that Jesus is present in the Tabernacle - a special place where they put the Eucharist - the actual body of Jesus Christ.

If you do this, you can ask this Jesus, who is present, to show you more fully his love for YOU.

He doesn't just love the world…he loves YOU! Drink it in. And let this be a belief that will be a foundation that will not be shaken.

Say: "GOD LOVES ME!"

Shout it out!

Knowing this will, in time, dispel your depression. All the nasty things that have occurred to you, all the bitter hassles were allowed to touch you so that you might lean more fully on the love of God.

Darcy when to a Catholic Church and was changed in the process. It was there she had a conversion of heart as she realized for the first time the love of God. All the hurt ultimately came to bring her into the arms of a loving God who loved her deeply and wanted her to trust him completely.

Why does God allow hurt? It is only ultimately to heal us, to take us to another level in our lives, to reach the mountain top struggling all the way, yet when we make it to the top there is unequalled joy.

Wow!

What love!

Now, think about your life and answer these questions:

1. Have you ever really been truly loved?
2. Who, without question, loves you today, without strings attached, no conditions?
3. Do you really believe that God loves you? If so, why? If not, why not?
4. What is keeping you from embracing his love?
5. Are you willing to go to a Catholic Church and spend time, in front of the crucifix, meditating on Christ's love for you?
6. How can this core belief of God's love dispel your depression?

Part 3

Door Number 3
OPENING YOUR SOUL

1

Opening The Door To God

———————

DARCY HAS GONE THROUGH TWO DOORS. The first door she went through broke her from the darkness of depression and brought her into a room filled with light and understanding. It was here that she began to reinterpret every event that happened to her.

It was life-changing!

Then she moved through the second door of love - choosing to accept and embrace the LOVE of God.

The changes she made in her life equalled a miracle.

Change is not always easy. For many, it is easy to sit in their chair of depression (again see door 1) rather than move into another sphere that is not familiar to them. Their depression is familiar. They are at home with it, since they have lived with it a long time. And too many nurses do this. After all they are professionals.   So they saunter on, covering their inner sadness.

Yet Darcy did not stay stuck in the darkness. Venturing out into the light took courage, and so too for you.

Hopefully you have come this far and taken giant leaps toward beating back your depression. Now, though, there is one final step, another door to go through that could change everything...for good.

Darcy walked through that open door to God. She knew he loved her. But she wanted more. She wanted to know him better on a friendship level deep within her soul.

Soul, you ask?

Why do we need God in our souls?

2

True Psychology

———————

WE ALL THINK WE KNOW WHAT PSYCHOLOGY IS. REALLY? Most do not know that the word comes from the Greek word "psyche," a word for the SOUL. Yet when you go to a psychologist or therapist, you will find that many have never studied the soul.

Because of this, most psychotherapists only take people part of the way to TOTAL recovery thus leaving their client only partially healed. They do not understand the true makeup of a person, that internal part that is left empty and alienated.

It is a shame that most universities where psychologists are trained never address this internal part of humanity. Why? It's simple. They refuse to study the soul, that very thing that psychology (SOULcology - the study of the soul) should be studying. But it is off limits at most universities. They avoid this study due to an antagonism against religion and any mention that brings God into the picture.

What happens? In avoiding the study of the soul, they take those suffering from depression only part of the way to healing and don't bring TOTAL Relief.

I wrote a series of books including workbooks and helpful "YES!" Cards to counter what too many therapists offer their clients - some even Christian, who are swept up in a more secular approach rather than leading each client on a pathway that will open their souls to God and his unmatched presence and love.

It was the great St. Augustine who said:

Thou hast made us for thyself and our hearts (souls) are restless until they find their rest in thee.

Jesus said:

Come to me all you who are weary and weighty difficulties and I will give you REST FOR YOUR SOULS.

Matt. 11

Soul rest. Now that's where real healing takes place.

Darcy had gone through door number one and learned how to think and act - reinterpreting each event so that she didn't feel bad and taking actions steps that reinforced those new thoughts.

Then she embraced the love of God accepting that any event that came her way, God allowed, in his love, to help her, not hurt her.

Now she needed to go through this final door and open her soul to God.

Darcy had come so far since being swamped by her depression when her fiancee left her just weeks before their marriage. Everything had turned dark spurred on by his rejection. She felt worthless and unworthy…until she saw how much God loved her and spoke clearly to her about her value, a value more than all the assets of the world, that value of her soul.

Darcy had discovered **TRUE PSYCHOLOGY** and her **SOUL** was being changed.

Book 3 of Dr. Paul's TOTAL Relief - Depression, goes a lot more in depth than this short work. You will learn the difference between an animal soul and a human soul and how that impacts you.

3

The Breath of God

DO YOU REALIZE THAT THE WORD "SOUL" CAN ALSO BE TRANSLATED "BREATH?" Amazing, isn't it that the one essential thing that gives us life is not food or water, but BREATH. This is the vital force that animates our bodies and is the seat of our emotions (feelings), will (action) and thoughts.

It is here that a person is distinguished from any other person, their uniqueness as designed by God.

It's interesting that we find in the creation account in Genesis that God BREATHED into Adam and Eve, and they became living SOULS.

No wonder so many relaxation techniques focus on the breath. Yet, even in this, they emphasize human breath rather than the divine breath of God breathing into our souls, bringing life, hope, joy and peace.

In my counseling, I have found that many who come to me have never fully spent time breathing in the presence and love of God. No wonder there is so much emptiness!

Years ago, while on a water skiing trip with some Christian teens, one of them challenged me to see if I could hold my breath as long as he. I accepted the challenge. He went under water and held his breath for a minute and a half. I did the same and bested his mark to a minute and 40 seconds.

He then held his breath for 2 minutes. I went under the water and held my breath for 2 1/2 minutes. He countered by 2 3/4 minutes.

Finally, I went under the water holding my breath. As I got to the 2 1/2 I felt my chest heaving, gasping for air. Then I heard them say 2 3/4 and then finally 3 minutes. I came out of the water desperately in need of air - to breathe again lest I die!

Breath. How vital it is. How necessary to living.

Yet, this essential, the breath of God, is neglected. We breathe oxygen but never this heavenly breath from a God who wants to breathe into us every day, every hour, every moment, his life.

You see, I was able to hold my breath for 3 minutes and was ready to die!

How long do we hold the breath of our souls without being nourished by God himself - a day, a week, a month, even years? No wonder there is so much depression among nurses, anxiety and fear. Very few are filling their souls with the breath of God.

How do we do this? Keep reading.

4

Filling The SOUL With God

———————

DARCY WAS MAKING GOOD PROGRESS TOWARD GETTING OVER HER DEPRESSION. Yet she had this final door to go through. She went to church and prayed some, but when I talked with her about the soul, she knew that she had a long way to go.

You need to take care of your soul, and you will take care of your depression. Why? Disturbance here will ripple through your whole person - your thoughts, actions and beliefs. Drink in the daily breath of God and, even through the hurts and disasters of life, you will be at peace with a joy that is unspeakable.

St. Peter said:

Though you have not seen him, you love him; and even though you do not see I'm now, you believe in him and are filled with an inexpressible and glorious joy...
I Peter 1:8-9

Did you get that…INEXPRESSIBLE AND GLORIOUS JOY. This is what all depressed people desire…JOY, an inner happiness that will not go away.

The secret: Being filled in your soul. When your soul if filled, this joy becomes automatic. And it comes…

> Not by just doing something
> But by being *with* SOMEONE

Christianity is not just a set of rules, beliefs and behaviors, but is essentially a RELATIONSHIP with God the Father, his Son, Jesus Christ and the Holy Spirit - all three want to fill your soul!

Awesome!

You see, **DOOR 1**, we learn how to think and act the right way, a way that changes how we feel.

In **DOOR 2**, we looked at our core beliefs and saw that the belief that will change our life the most is embracing the LOVE of God. He is never out to hurt us but help us (though that sometimes hurts). He is always out to make us better. His love insures that.

In **DOOR 3,** we are brought to see our most essential self - our soul and learning how to breathe in the breath of God.

His breath gives life abundant, life to the full, resulting in inexpressible, indescribable, unspeakable, unfathomable glorious, magnificent, dazzling, awesome, remarkable, sensational, gratifying JOY!

It is here that his thoughts become our thoughts and his ways become our ways. There becomes a blending of our natures as we share in his divine life.

Some circles of Christianity call this the EXCHANGED LIFE - he in us and we in him.

It was the Psalmist who said in Psalm 23:

> *The LORD is my Shepherd*
> *I shall not have any need*
> *He makes me lie down*
> *by quiet thirst quenching streams*
> ***HE RESTORES MY SOUL***

Darcy asked: "How does this happen? What can I do to restore my soul, to fill it so that I don't feel this emptiness anymore?

"One of the answers is found in the Gospel of John," I said.
I then went on and related this information.

In the Gospel of John Jesus asked a couple of men,

"What do you want?"

This is one of the greatest questions that was ever asked.

King Solomon was told by God that he would give him "whatever he wanted." And, to paraphrase his answer, he asked that he might have a deep relationship with God, that he could hear him with the ears of his heart.

When Jesus asked these two men this question, they gave the GREATEST answer one could give, an answer in line with King Solomon's wish. These men said:

"We want to know where you live - where you abide."

Now on the surface this doesn't seem very deep. But these men were not asking for Jesus' address, but instead they were looking for the opportunity to spend time with him - at his place, his residence, his home.

They wanted to be AT HOME WITH JESUS.

So Jesus took them, these 2 men, only 2 men, to his home. And they started a revolution that changed the world.

Within a day these 2 men reached another 2 men, and on and on. By the time Jesus died there were over 500 men and women, then 3,000, then 8,000 and soon there were over 50,000 in Jerusalem who had become followers of Jesus.

How did it happen?

Two guys who wanted to spend time with Jesus.

That's all. They wanted to be JOHN 15 men (read this chapter - it's amazing). They wanted to abide with Christ.

You see, you can't spend time with Jesus and nothing else happens. In that quiet time with him you are transformed, made into one of his revolutionaries, a disciple who becomes an IMPACT person, a nurse who is radiant with a joy that impacts others.

But, IT ALL STARTS WITH TIME WITH JESUS.

You start with Jesus - listening to him in the Gospels, or in the Psalms, or the book of Philippians, or any other book of the Bible, journaling, praying, opening your heart to his desires, confessing your sin, sharing with him you deepest concerns.

It is in this time that you become friends that meet each day. And it is from this time together that something happens to you. You are changed deep within your soul and want to impact others.

So…WHAT DO YOU WANT?

Darcy said: "I want more of Jesus."

"Then," I responded, "spend time with him in Scripture (read the Gospels), in prayer, and, if Catholic, before the Blessed Sacrament, seeing Jesus in the bread and wine and receiving the TOTAL Christ, both spiritually and physically (in bread and wine which is transformed into his body and blood).

Too many Christians only receive Jesus spiritually. And this is great! Keep doing that. But also consider what the early Christians did, received him also physically in the bread and wine.

Jesus did not come just spiritually. The incarnation means he took upon himself true flesh. The real Jesus is not just a spirit, but a body and spirit. Receive both of them (body, blood, soul and divinity) in the Eucharist in the Catholic Church. It can make all the difference.

The TOTAL JESUS comes to rest in your soul.

Next, I gave Darcy this outline of how to read Scripture in a special way, a way that opens the SOUL to Jesus.

Lectio Divina

Lectio Divina is a slow, prayerful, meditative, contemplative approach to the Scriptures. Lectio Divina means "divine reading." It is a very old practice in the Church and goes back to St. Benedict in the 6th century. There are rules you must follow to practice Lectio Divina. It is an approach to Holy Scripture that is:

1. **SLOW.** You are not out to read an entire section, chapter or even a paragraph. You go word by word, drinking in the meaning, pausing as you observe this word of God to you. You don't want to miss anything. You have prayed: "Open my eyes that I may see wondrous things out of your word" (Psalm 119), and you believe that this will come to pass. You are centering on HIM, your creator, your master, your intimate friend.

It may take you a week, two weeks, a month to get through a chapter. But that's OK. It's not how much of the bible you get through that counts but how much of the bible gets into you. This is a treasure hunt where you are looking under every word for that special treasure God has for you. It is like squeezing an orange, desiring to get out all the juice, the sweetness into your soul. You are seeking to merge your thoughts with HIS thoughts. So you quiet your mind, find a place where you can leisurely loiter in the presence of the God who wants to embrace you, guide you, and be your friend.

2. **PRAYERFUL.** It is here in the Scriptures that we meet face to face with God. He wants to enfold us into a deep relationship with him. So we pray, "Come Father, come Holy Spirit, come Lord Jesus and meet me as I drink in your precious words." It is in this process that we find that Jesus will "open our minds to understand the Scriptures," like he did those early two disciples on the road to Emmaus. So as we read the Holy Scriptures, we are always praying, communicating with the God who gave us his word.

The Scriptures are like a telescope that bring us into the presence of God. Too often people study the telescope, take it apart, know all about how it functions and works. And that may be good, but the ultimate purpose of a telescope is to bring a person into the presence of the stars. So too the Scriptures. You can study them, memorize them, read them, tear them apart, but until you let them bring you into the presence of Jesus, you are not using them the way they were designed.

This is why, when we open this sacred book, we pray and keep on praying. The words of Scripture are not ordinary words. They are powerful, explosive, life changing. And we cannot come with human understanding and think we will grasp what these words mean. We must tune our ears to the writer of these words, God himself, talking with him, and letting him talk with us.

3. **MEDITATIVE.** Here we are ruminating, marinating, chewing, rolling over the words of Scripture in our minds and hearts. During this time we are talking with God and letting him talk with us. The "ears on our hearts" like Solomon, are attentive, ready to receive insight, the kind that produces a "burning in our hearts," like it did on those two early disciples with Jesus. At this point we begin direct dialogue with God, interacting, drinking, eating, breathing in his words, letting our souls consume them, this spiritual nourishment that is vital to our spiritual existence. God is becoming our friend in an intimacy that cannot be described, so deep it is, so close, so loving. We share with him our deepest desires, our hopes, our dreams, our pain, our doubts, our confidence in him. And we listen, drinking in his words in the moment, *rhema,* hot bread for the soul that results in joy and inner gladness.

King David in Psalm 1, talks about ruminating on the Scriptures day and night. I recommend people memorize sections of Scriptures as they work through them, words of God that they can sift through in their minds and hearts through the day. Like a cow chewing its cud, we can chew on the Word of God, slowly, meditatively, getting out of it all the nourishment that is needed for that moment.

4. **CONTEMPLATIVE.** You are swept into a place of total reverence, praise and joy. You drink it in, not saying anything, not listening at this point, just lingering, resting in HIS presence.   There is a total silence, yet a communication that goes beyond words taking us into infinity, into the realm of God, into his throne room, the holy of holies. It is like two lovers who embrace without saying any words. The moment has swept them into an encounter of their souls. So too with God. He is in us, we in him, in that infinite, finite embrace.

It is like mouth to mouth resuscitation. We receive his life. At this point we may hear the groans of the Holy Spirit that St. Paul talks about in Romans 8, uttering words that we cannot understand.   It is awesome, breathtaking, magnificent, overwhelming and absolutely necessary if we are going to get back to the Garden of Eden where we lost this great gift, communing with and embracing our creator.

This brings about the change we need, a change that breathes into us HIS life.

Making sure that Darcy had sufficient tools so that she could open her soul to the breath of God, I also gave her this helpful approach to opening any Scriptural text.

THE FIVE QUESTIONS Method
TO READING THE SCRIPTURE
(Can be used with the daily readings)

When you read a specific Scripture or focus on the daily readings like The WORD Among Us, MAGNIFICAT, or others, ask the following five questions. They will help you to dig deeper and allow you to benefit greatly with your time with God. It is best to read a paragraph or two as you do this.

1. What is a **KEY WORD,** words or phrase that stands out when I read this passage? Look it up in the dictionary to get its clear meaning or use biblehub.com.

2. In a **SENTENCE** or two, what is the passage talking about?

3. Can I **ILLUSTRATE** what the passage is talking about in my own life or in the life of another?

4. What is Jesus **ASKING ME TO DO** in response to this passage?

5. If Jesus were standing before me right now (and he is!) and asked me: **"WHAT DO YOU WANT** me to do for you?" What would I say?

Write these answers down in your journal. It's life changing!

Jesus stands at the door of your life, your soul and wants to come in. Listen to him as he says:

Look. I stand at the door of your soul and would like to come in. I won't force myself in. You must invite me into your life. If you do, I will come in and feed you in a way that you have never been fed before. You will delight in my presence and your soul will finally be at peace, and experience hope and joy.

5

The Miracle of Praise

WHEN YOU DISCOVER TRUE PSYCHOLOGY AND THE VALUE OF YOUR SOUL, you will never be the same. You will begin to develop a relationship with your creator, the one who started the human race by BREATHING INTO THEM, and they became living souls.

As a nurse, once you understand the magic of this, this depth that is missed in most therapy sessions in the world, you will begin to come to a place where true healing will occur. Your soul will be finally liberated to become all the creator intended - and that will free it to find, as the Psalmist said:

PLEASURES FOR EVER!

Psalm 16

When you begin to feel this joy, your heart will begin to sing praises to God. He, your eternal lover, has satisfied your soul and you lift up your hands, clap, shout, blast the trumpet as you praise him.

Look at all the praise Psalms in Scripture. They come from hearts that are full and overflowing with gratitude to God.

There is something magical that happens to you when you begin to praise God. A power is released in your mind and emotions that cannot be matched by any other exercise.

People take drugs to imitate this kind of feeling. And they may get it for a moment or two. Then, back to the drugs for another hit - hoping, grasping, longing for a joy that will never end.

But in God is FULLNESS of joy. Living in HIS PRESENCE, breathing in his nature is all that is needed to release the human spirit to fly high, to move beyond the grips of depression and despair.

Praise.

There is so much **power** in it.

Praise the LORD (Psalm 150)

Hallelujah!
Praise God in His sanctuary
Praise Him in the firmament of his power
Praise God for His mighty acts
Praise Him according to His abundant greatness
Praise Him with the blast of the horn
Praise Him with the psaltery and harp
Praise Him with the timbrel and dance
Praise Him with stringed instruments and the pipe
Praise him with the loud-sounding cymbals
Praise Him with the clanging cymbals
Let every thing that hath breath
PRAISE THE LORD!
Hallelujah!

You may also want to praise God in music. Sing to him. Put on some CD's or any other way to get music into the room, into your soul. As you play, you can dance, clap your hands, grab two pot lids and clang them together.

Go wild!

Let yourself loose and praise the LORD!

6

Review The Doors, Your Steps To Success

Let's review:

THERE ARE THREE DOORS YOU NEED TO GO THROUGH AS A NURSE if you want to bring healing to your depression.

Door 1 - Getting Unstuck. Here you move off the chair of depression, out of the darkness into the light. You discover that you were making yourself depressed by the way you interpreted various events that happened to you. You learned that if you changed your INTERPRETATIONS, you could change how you felt. You tried it, and it works!

You then went on and changed your actions - breathing, standing up straight, going for a walk, smiling, even laughing. These actions helped your brain to accept the new interpretations you were making about the negative events that happened to you.

Door 2 - Embracing God's LOVE. You saw that all your thoughts flowed from foundational beliefs, and the greatest foundational belief is God's LOVE FOR **YOU**. You don't have to earn it. He loves you no matter what you have ever done. He can't help it, because he is pure, personal love. When you embrace his love it will change everything.

Door 3 - Opening your SOUL to God. This is where the real healing takes place. God wants to breathe his life into your soul, and when he does, you experience a healing to the depth that is unimaginable. His life becomes yours. There is that unusual exchange where you share each other's lives.

It's a miracle!

Impossible? Not at all. In fact it is promised by God himself and has been experienced by millions of people over the years.

Darcy walked through all three doors. And now, today, her life is full and fulfilled. There is a depth of satisfaction that nothing else ever brought her.

And now those doors are open for you.

Walk through them.

Allow the life of God to penetrate the center of your existence.

And enjoy a life that is like Darcy's…

FULL AND FULFILLED WITH AN INNER
SATISFACTION THAT NEVER ENDS.

A Prayer For You To Pray…Now

Dear LORD GOD
My FATHER
My Creator
My Hope.
You proved your love for me
through your Son, Jesus Christ,
And now it is your desire to restore my soul.
As a nurse struggling with depression
I come to you to
Find new hope and joy in YOU.
I let you into my soul
Fully
Without reservation
Drinking in your presence
Now and forever.

Amen

Don't Stop With This Book Alone. You are on a journey to heal your depression.

GO ALL THE WAY and get healing by using Dr. Paul's followup books that will help you find healing - TOTAL healing.

DR. PAUL'S 10 DAY CURE
DEPRESSION DOOR 1, 2 and 3

Congratulations!

You have taken a step in the right direction to overcome your depression and find lasting joy, again, or maybe for the first time in your life.

Though the **99¢ Cure for depression** was complete in itself, you need to now make sure that you go through each door, MASTERING EACH STEP so that you can finally go through DOOR 3 to freedom!

You may have read the book, liked what you read, but you haven't yet taken the necessary steps to cure your depression.

This 10 DAY CURE, step by step plan, will assist you so that you can be successful.

There are three great books that will take you step by step to find a cure.

You can get these on my website, **DrPaulYoung.com** Look under "SHOP".

DR. PAUL'S *YES!*
CURE CARDS
DEPRESSION DOOR 1, 2 and 3

YES! is a powerful word. Don't you like it when someone says, "Yes," to you? It's positive, decisive, and confident.

YES!

"YES," has the ring of certainty to it. There is no doubt, no disagreement. The action is final…YES! You are in agreement, you will do it… NOW!

YES CURE CARDS are **MEDICINE FOR THE SOUL,** to help you heal, to bring hope and cheer to a soul that has lost its way.

For years now, since the late 70's, I have been using these kinds of cards to help people blast through their depression, anxiety, fear, anger, and a host of other maladies.

After all, when you go see the doctor and you are sick, he writes out a prescription for you, a prescription designed to make you whole again.   That's what these **YES CURE CARDS** are - prescriptions that are actually MEDICINE FOR THE SOUL.

I know they help, and are worth their weight in gold.   Use them everyday.   Use them often throughout the day to break old habits of thinking and acting, of believing and receiving the life-changing breath of God in your soul.

YES CURE CARDS can change the direction of a thought and turn it into another direction.   That's why they are so powerful.   It's a simple affirmation that will turn the course of your thoughts, actions and beliefs from one direction to another - FAST.

You can purchase these on **<u>DrPaulYoung.com</u>** and look for "SHOP".

TRUE STORIES

If you want true stories of people and how I helped them through their depression and the exciting breakthroughs they made, see my ***Dr. Paul's TOTAL Relief*** series on my website at DrPaulYoung.com.

It's magical!

1. Or you might want to read a most unusual book, ***Potato Salad For The Depressed Soul.*** This is one of those books that will catch you by surprise - the way it will revamp your thinking as you make potato salad.

2. There is also a book in the Bible that has "JOY" in it more than any other, the book of Philippians. I took this book and personalized it, writing as if it was written to YOU. It has helped many people who are struggling with depression and anxiety to find hope and joy again. You can download it to your phone or other device and carry this wonderful message from God, personally to you. It's called: ***The Personalized Bible - Philippians***. Go to DrPaulYoung.com

3. I have another book written to those who lost so much through the fires that swept through Santa Rosa, California with over 5,000 homes burned to the ground in just a couple hours.

We were chased out of our home for 13 days - frightened, anxious and all that one experiences during a time of horrific destruction. The book's name is **Guaranteed Recovery After a Loss.**

You may have lost a mate, gone through a divorce, lost a lot of money or a personal friend who will no longer see you. So much loss. How do you deal with it? This book will help. It's short yet powerful.   Again, you can find it on DrPaulYoung.com

4. My most unusual book, ***Dr. Paul's FEELING GOOD ToolKit*** has hundreds of charts that will help you reinterpret any event and add actions that will break the back of depression and anxiety.

I write books that help, are practical, not theoretical, with contents that have been proven to release people from depression, anxiety and other destructive emotions.

Dr. Paul J. Young

Education:

University of California, Fresno, B.A in English

Dallas Theological Seminary, Th.M (Masters in Theology)

Biola University, Doctorate of Ministry with emphasis on psychology (working with Talbot School of Theology, Rosemead School of Psychology and other schools)

Dr. Paul Joseph Young

…helped grow one of the largest churches in the Dallas/Ft. Worth area as its pastor, working with thousands of people, developing his skills both as a minister, communicator and a counselor, working with hundreds of people and developing his unique therapy techniques.

For seven years he was C.E.O. of Community Bible Study International, working in over 60 countries of the world, sharing his message of hope and joy. He held seminars on depression, anxiety, stress, fear, anger, and a host of other topics, seeking to bring healing to the thousands in need.

Dr. Paul's communication skills has made him a favorite speaker around the world. He lives with his wife and best friend, Diane. They have five children and 14 grandchildren.

More than anything, Dr. Paul lives to help people find the joyful life they deserve.

This is a

<u>DRPAULYOUNG.COM</u>

Publication

____